ISM Working Paper No. 19

Jens K. Perret

On the Gender Performance Gap in Economics Education - A Comparison of German Public and Private Universities

Perret, Jens K: On the Gender Performance Gap in Economics Education - A Comparison of German Public and Private Universities

© 2022 ISM
Alle Rechte vorbehalten

Herstellung und Verlag: BoD – Books on Demand,
Norderstedt
ISBN 978-3-7568-8518-3

ISM - International School of Management gGmbH
Otto-Hahn-Str. 19 · 44227 Dortmund
www.ism.de
Tel.: 0231.975139-0 · Fax: 0231.975139-39
ism.dortmund@ism.de

Perret, Jens K.: On the Gender Performance Gap in Economics Education - A Comparison of German Public and Private Universities, Dortmund und Norderstedt, BoD, 2022 (Working Paper ; 19)
ISBN 978-3-7568-8518-3

Contents

Perret, Jens K.:
On the Gender Performance Gap in Economics Education -
A Comparison of German Public and Private Universities

List of Tables

Abstract

Broad ranges of studies have discussed the difference in performance between men and women in relation to their economics education. The German perspective with its particular tertiary education system and decade long history of gender equality movements, however, remain under researched. By implementing two data sets, a German public university and a German private university of applied sciences, this study aims to provide to the existing literature in this regard. The datasets have been used to test, in a nationwide sample, potential gender differences in the outcome of exams in basic economics. By consisting of a total of more than 9,000 observations over nine years or 18 semesters and seven locations across Germany, the study constructs a comprehensive view of the German academic landscape.

The results as well as robustness checks show that gender effects are marginal at best. Additionally, it has been shown that no significant differences exist across the difference forms of universities. The results of this broadband sample lead to the conjecture that in Germany, independent of the type of university, over the last decades gender equality in economics education has been consolidated and any observed effects are due to external factors alone.

1   Introduction

Since the 1960s, the question has been raised whether men and women perform differently in the field of economics and related fields like politics (Mondak/Anderson 2004) or finance (Myers et al. 2018) when performing in economic aptitude tests or participating in final exams of introductory university courses (Siegfried 1979). The discussion started at roughly the same time as issues of gender inequality, e.g. in payment and outcomes, as a problem entered the societal spotlight as well as academia in general.

In addition to asking about the existence of differences between the genders[1], studies have also inquired about the reasons behind those differences (Thompson 2012). In contrast to early studies that already had to condition their results to the type of questions asked, more recent ones like Chan/Kennedy (2002), Ballard/Johnson (2005) and Johnson et al. (2014) often fail to provide significant evidence of difference at all. This is despite the fact that a number of these studies differentiate for the type of questions (usually analytical vs. non-analytical) as well.

---

[1] Note that in this study the terms gender and biological sex are to be understood as synonyms. The idea of gender as a social construct while offering interesting insights of its own is considered irrelevant in the context of this study.

Perret, Jens K.:
On the Gender Performance Gap in Economics Education -
A Comparison of German Public and Private Universities

The commonality of most studies is their focus on specifically designed tests[2] answered in artificial situations by students sampled from the student body of a single university[3]. In addition, sample sizes rarely exceed 200 participants[4]. From a pure study design perspective, all studies should thus be treated with some skepticism, however well the implemented tests are constructed.

In more recent years, studies started focusing on the reasons behind different outcomes for men and women (MacDowell et al. 1977; Hirschfeld et al. 1995; Thompson 2012). Accounting for biases resulting from artificial testing situations Hirschfeld et al. (1995) focus on real-world situations using real test results, i.e. the General Record Examination (GRE) where the participants were not aware that they were studied, thus behaving as naturally as any official test allows. The study by Wuthisatian (2020) is of particular interest since it considers performance in proctored online exams, an exam type, that became increasingly more important, not the least due to the COVID-19 motivated lockdowns of universities and an increase in distance learning programs.

Most studies focus on the US. The studies by Makridou-Bossiou (2006) (Greece) and Marin/Rosa-Garcia (2011) (Spain) are among the select few focusing on the European situation. Up to this point, the studies by Kaiser (2020) and Oberrauch/Kaiser (2020), focusing on secondary schools, are the only ones broaching the topic for Germany. Considering the German tertiary education system no study has been realized as of yet.

In Germany compared to the US, no central national placement test like the GRE exists. Additionally, the German tertiary education system as such is not homogeneous insofar as the relevant institutions can be divided into universities and universities of applied science, the first having a more academic orientation and the second has a more practical one. Both types of universities exist as publicly or privately operated institutions with different levels of governmental accreditation. The second section provides a more in-depth description of the German tertiary education system.

In the course of the present paper data, for a set of students from a public German university (GU) as well as for a private German university of applied sciences (GUAS) has been collected with regard to the results of the first (GU) or second (GUAS) semester courses in economics. As the GUAS data has been collected from the six different campuses, in total data for seven German regions (Wuppertal, Cologne, Dortmund, Hamburg, Frankfurt, Munich, Stuttgart) have been considered, spanning a considerable geographical area (acknowledging the overrepresentation of cities in North Rhein-Westphalia) allotting this study a decent level of representativeness.

---

[2] The implemented tests like the *Test of Understanding in College Economics*, the *Test of Economics Understanding* or the *Test of Economic Literacy* are among the most commonly implemented tests.
[3] Only studies like Attiyeh/Lumsden 1971 or Lumsden/Scott 1987 consider a national sample.
[4] The studies by Ferber et al. 1983, Lumsden/Scott 1987 and Heath 1989 use sample sizes of roughly 550, 1300-1500 and 3000 (600) and are among those with the largest overall samples. Studies conducted during the 1970s and early 1980s on average report sample sizes between 100 to 200.

The data in both contexts consists of all students for a period of 18 semesters or 9 years. As the same time frame has been used in both cases, in a second part of the analysis both data sets can be pooled contrasting the two types of institutions.

Following the discussion of the topic through the historic and recent literature, the analysis for the two data sets in carried out, the study results are discussed, and respective conclusions developed.

2 The Role of Gender in Economics - A Literature Review

The studies by Bach/Saunders (1965) and Bach/Saunders (1966) are among the first to analyze gender differences in the course of economics education.

Siegfried (1979) summarizes the first one and a half decade of research in this area. Summarizing the different studies, Siegfried (1979) argues that in roughly two out of three studies men report a better understanding of economics but only in one out of three they are better at acquiring new skills.

A more recent study by Johnson et al. (2014) comes to a similar result that in roughly two out of three studies men report better results, but in only about one out of three these results are also significant.

The studies that do not find any differences include Kelley (1975), Buckles/Freeman (1983), Watts (1987), Rhine (1989) or more recently Chan/Kennedy (2002) and Ballard/Johnson (2005).

The broader context of most of the earlier studies is a discussion of the discriminatory nature of economics education as practiced at the time. They also focus on dimensions of a more gender-neutral economics education. They thus relate to questions like the one asked by Becker/Watts (2001) and more recently Roach (2014) whether the teaching style in economics per se has to change. While the effects on the lecturer's gender on student performance has been studied (Chudgar/Sankar 2008; Antecol et al. 2015), as of yet no study considered the effect different teaching styles have on gender difference in exam performance among students.

With some studies having been conducted at the high school level, Hirschfeld et al. (1995), Ferber et al. (1983), Lumsden/Scott (1987), Gohmann/Spector (1989) or Watts/Lynch (1989) among others are conducted on a college level.

The reasons behind gender differences that are regularly discussed center on the assumption that women are better in regard to qualitative essay questions Lumsden/Scott (1987) whereas men are better in regard to quantitative analytical questions[5]. Ferber et al. (1983), however, could show that there do not exist any significant differences in regard to essays. Chan/Kennedy (2002) show that if multiple choice and essay questions are combined, no significant differences exist.

---

[5] Hedges/Nowell 1995 report on the gender gap in mathematics.

Perret, Jens K.:
On the Gender Performance Gap in Economics Education -
A Comparison of German Public and Private Universities

The reasons underlying these approaches stems from studies proposing a higher interest and a stronger inclination towards economics and mathematics in men in general (Tonin/Wahba 2015). This argument is shared at least indirectly by Siegfried (1979), Ferber et al. (1983), Lumsden/Scott (1987), Watts (1987), Soper/Walstad (1988), Walstad/Soper (1989) and Watts/Lynch (1989). Heath (1989) additionally argues that given the opportunity, men are more likely to choose economics courses in their studies. In contrast, Arnold/Wietske (2014) argue that, if women do chose economics classes they are more intrinsically motivated than men. Ballard/Johnson (2005) show that the gender gap becomes insignificant if control variables for expectations and background knowledge are introduced.

Finally, following Burns et al. (2012) women are more risk averse; with risk taking impacting the outcome of tests.

The present study aims to contribute to this discussion by providing an insight into the situation in Germany and by implementing a broader data set than most previous studies. Considering recent studies Chan/Kennedy (2002) and the ongoing debate of previously listed inconclusive discussions concerning reasons for differing results, this study abstains from formulating a pre-defined research hypothesis. Following an open exploratory approach, the research question is posed: Do differences between men and women exist across and within different institutions of tertiary education in Germany in the field of basic economics.

3   The German Tertiary Education System

A significant share of the studies presented in the previous section relate to the US education system. To ease comparisons between these studies and the present one, this section introduces the basic structure of the German tertiary education system.

Three major characteristics can be used to distinguish between the different institutions: government accreditation, private vs. public operation and field of focus (universities vs. universities of applied sciences).

Aside from public institutions, privately operated ones may refer to themselves as universities, academies or other designations, only state-accredited institutions can provide their students with generally accepted degrees that attest to a certain quality in education. This accreditation takes place in two stages. First, the institution itself needs to be accredited. The *Wissenschaftsrat / German Council of Science and Humanities* performs this service of evaluation for the German government. Different levels of governmental accreditation are possible, mainly differing in the duration the accreditation remains valid.

In the second stage, all study programs are accredited on a regular basis. This process applies to public and private institutions alike. Only students having finished an accredited study program can officially carry the title.

The second distinction is between public and private institutions. While the number of private universities in Germany is limited, it is mostly universities of applied sciences that are privately operated. Private institutions can either have a non-profit or for-profit orientation. The main difference between private and public institutions can be seen in the study fees charged. While public institutions have no study fees as such, they levy a fee to cover organizational costs. Overall study fees at a private institution are between five to twenty times as high as those at a public institution resulting on average in smaller student numbers and class sizes.

The third and final distinction is between universities and universities of applied sciences. While universities are considered more academically oriented, fostering careers in research and development and educating future academics, universities of applied sciences are more practically oriented. Only a very limited number of universities of applied sciences are allowed to awards doctoral degrees. Most universities of applied sciences, in particular in the private sector have a strong focus on economics and business administration or related fields.

A further distinction into for-profit and non-profit private institutions exists, but remains irrelevant in a German context of this study, since education as such might alone be marginally impacted by the distinction and a majority of 96. 4% of all German universities (private and public, universities and universities of applied sciences) are non-profit (UniRank 2022). The only difference might result from the fact that the payment structure of lecturers differs in for-profit and non-profit institutions attracting differently motivated lecturers. Nevertheless, this aspect is already accounted for by a differentiation into private and public universities.

4 Data Sources and Methodology

To answer the underlying research question, two unique data sets have been combined. For the GU, results from a first semester course in macroeconomics have been collected for a total of 18 consecutive semesters starting with the winter semester 2007-2008. For the same period, data for the GUAS has been available. Both institutions considered in this study are state-accredited, and both data sets result from students in accredited study programs.

Due to a change in the mode of examination at the GUAS, first semester exams in macroeconomics had to be replaced in later semesters by exams on basic economics (including micro- and macroeconomics) written in the second semester. Since students were not forced to switch study programs once they started, no clear cut as to when one type ended and the other began has been possible. As some students used the opportunity to write the exam at a later date or had to repeat one of the exams, no definitive distinction with regard to specific semesters is possible.

Perret, Jens K.:
On the Gender Performance Gap in Economics Education -
A Comparison of German Public and Private Universities

In the GUAS data set, gender has been explicitly stated and no additional processing of the data set is required. In the GU data set, gender is not explicitly stated and is assigned based on the first names of the students. This leads to the problem that not all names can unambiguously be identified as male or female, i.e. Robin, in these cases the corresponding students have been removed from the data set. With foreign students (mainly of Turkish or Chinese origin) only those whose names could be unambiguously assigned to a gender were considered all others were removed from the data set. This process removed less than 1% of all students from the data set, so that any bias resulting from it can be precluded.

The final GU data set consists of 5,683 observations, while the GUAS data set consists of 3,794 participants. Of the 5,683 GU students a total of 2,918 (51.4%) are women and of the 3,794 GUAS students a total of 2,204 (58.1%) are women. Both data sets thus consist of a sufficient number of observations and report a suitable split with regard to the main impact factor, gender. Note that each case in the data set represents a single exam, with students being able to write up to three exams at both institutions. The corresponding problem with multiple measures is noted at this point. Considering that only 9.8% of all students in the GU data set had to use a second or third try (detailed data in this regard has not been available for the GUAS data set), potential biases resulting from this can be considered minor and will not separately discussed.

Even though the exams providing the GU data set have been created by the same lecturers, additional information on the semester the exam is taken is collected, accounting for biases resulting from different exam compositions. Using information on the semester in their overall studies, a student takes the exam and how often he already took part in the exam allows for a measure of the experience of students in regard to taking the exams and economics education in general.

Finally, the data set allows to account for of the study program the students are enrolled in. Since the data set encompasses students from economics, business administration and the social sciences as well as students of business mathematics and engineering, this control is of importance.

The exams providing the GUAS data set, even though pooling two types of exam structures, have been comparable across the time horizon of this study in regard to the queried content.

While in this data set, it is not possible to control for the specific semester the year the students started with their studies are known. Additionally, it is not possible to account for the different study programs, nevertheless differences across study programs are negligible since they all focus on the broad field of management and all students are faced with the same entrance exams and take the same introductory mathematics and statistic lectures. All students thus start their economics education with the same level (at least theoretically) of previously acquired background knowledge and mathematical skills. The GUAS during the study horizon has been active with six different campuses, and it is possible to control for the campus where the students took the exam. Since at each campus there is a different lecturer teaching and grading the exams, even though these exams are the same, this control avoids regional biases.

It needs to be mentioned that the GUAS data set only reported students who passed their exams. All information regarding students who failed the exam had been omitted before extraction from the data management system and is not available for analysis. Finally, the cultural background and thus differently learning styles are partially accounted for in the GU data set. Since all names are available verbatim they are assignment to one of four groups. The first group covers those students where the first and the surname have a middle eastern connotation (dominated by names of Turkish origin), the second group summarizes those students where the names suggest an Asian background and the third group summarizes all other students with foreign language names. Note, that the third groups except for a single digit number of exceptions includes Eastern European students or those from countries of the former Soviet Union. The fourth and final group includes all those students where no distinct foreign cultural background can be detected via the name. Since this assignment is highly speculative the results are only used in an additional robustness check but not as part of the full analysis.

Since grades are measured on an ordinal scale, if failed exams are included, an ordered logit regression is used throughout the following analysis; noting that in the GUAS data set as well as in the reduced version of the GU data set (excluding failed exams) a linear regression is also valid.

5 Gender Differences

In a first step both data sets are considered separately. Since different controls were available for the two cases, treating them separately allows for getting the most insights from each one.

Model 1, as reported in Table 1 and Table 2, includes only the gender variable, generating a baseline scenario. In both cases the coefficients are positive, implying that those studies are correct that propose that men achieve better results; however, only in the GU case this effect is significantly different from zero. Thus, even in the base version, differences are marginal at best. With R^2 values of below 0.002 it can be conjectured that gender plays a less than marginal role when trying to explain academic performance in economics.

In Model 2 and 3 an increasing number of controls are introduced, providing a robustness check for the baseline scenario of Model 1. Here the GU data set is of particular

Perret, Jens K.:
On the Gender Performance Gap in Economics Education -
A Comparison of German Public and Private Universities

interest, as aside from the experience of the student,[6] it has been possible to control for the study program the student is enrolled in and in model 3 the semester the exam has been taken. In particular, the semester dummy variables lead to a significant increase in explanatory power with an R^2 of 0.175 and an almost tenfold increase in the F statistic signifying that the difficulty of the exam or rather the difference in exams is a central explanatory aspect. Including the semester dummies also halves the effect of the gender variable, rendering it insignificant.

The results of an ordered logistic regression (assuming that the marks are essentially only ordinal in nature) are presented as Model 4 in the last column. Here the R^2 statistic is replaced by Nagelkerke's Pseudo R^2 and the F-test by a χ^2-test. In essence they mirror the results from Model 3, which might result from an even distribution of points across those who failed their exam.

Finally, considering only those students who passed their exams[7], results in Model 3*. The main insight compared to Model 3 can be found in an additional decrease of the coefficient for the gender variable. In conclusion, gender may play a very marginal role in passing the exam while it is negligible in determining the end result assuming the exam has been passed. Model 3* is also the model that could be used in comparison with the GUAS data set since there data per se is only available for those students that passed their exams.

Table 1 Regression Results – GU
Source: Own presentation

Variables	Model 1	Model 2	Model 3	Model 3*	Model 4
Gender	0.252***	0.208*	0.119	0.039	0.082
	(0.083)	(0.11)	(0.101)	(0.099)	(0.061)
Semester of Student		-0.035	-0.018	0.011	-0.013
		(0.26)	(0.024)	(0.023)	(0.015)
2. Try		-0.425**	-0.546***	-0.587***	-0.362***
		(0.196)	(0.190)	(0.190)	(0.116)
3. Try		-0.436	-0.625	-1.037**	-0.290
		(0.479)	(0.461)	(0.43)	(0.279)
Dummies Program	-	+	+	+	+
Dummies Semester	-	-	+	+	+
Constant	3.946***	4.455***	5.314***	5.682***	-
	(0.58)	(0.91)	(0.141)	(0.133)	-
R^2 (Nagelkerke)	0.002	0.009	0.175	0.129	0.178
F / χ^2	9.157***	4.435***	40.398***	23.599***	668,802***

---

[6] Experience is measured by the semester the student already has been studying and the number of times he already took part in the exam.

[7] This step is considered to assure comparability with the GUAS data set where information on failed exams was omitted before extraction.

In the GUAS data set, information on the study programs and the semester dummy variables is not available. Thus, in addition to students' experience[8] the location of the campus the student took the exam at[9] and the year of enrollment are considered as control variables. Model 1 again is the baseline model without any controls, while Model 2 introduces the student-based controls and location dummies. Model 3 for the GU data set introduces additional time dummies. Since the data set is already limited to those exams graded 4.0 or better, a respective Model 3* or Model 4 is not required. Models 1 through 3 in a direct comparison to Table 1 report unanimously worse R^2 statistics. Nevertheless, the F-test (mainly due to the large number of participants) remains highly significant throughout.

While the gender variable becomes barely significant in Model 2, in contrast to Table 1 it remains more or less at the same size throughout all three Model 3, being unaffected by the inclusion of additional control variables.

As an additional robustness check based on the cultural backgrounds of the students, as motivated in the methodology section, is conducted. While the flaws of the assignment process are acknowledged, it can be stated that this additional information only marginally impacts the estimation results ($R^2 = 0.004$). Looking at the different groups it can be seen that only those students with a Middle Eastern background reports significantly different results, with an average mark approximately 0.21 worse than the rest of the observed students. Disregarding significance in all three groups the outcomes of the exams are worse than for the "German" students.

Table 2 Regression Results – GUAS
Source: Own presentation

Variables	Model 1	Model 2	Model 3
Gender	0.118	0.128*	0.120
	(0.077)	(0.076)	(0.075)
Semester of Student		0.32***	0.106
		(0.057)	(0.108)
Begin in Summer		0.021	0.052
		(0.094)	(0.093)
English Trail		-0.395*	-0.291
		(0.221)	(0.222)
Dummies Location	-	+	+
Dummies Year	-	-	+
Constant	4.882***	4.075***	4.421***
	(0.050)	(0.144)	(0.203)
R^2	0.001	0.032	0.057
F	2.382	13.719***	10.344***

---

[8] Measured in this case via the semester of the first official chance to take part in the exam. Anecdotal evidence shows that for many of students, this also is the first time by which they take part in the exam.

[9] Note that the data set is based on a private university of applied science with at the time six different campuses across Germany.

Perret, Jens K.:
On the Gender Performance Gap in Economics Education -
A Comparison of German Public and Private Universities

Again, this strengthens the argument that any gender effect might only be a statistical artifact created via the impact of outside factors. Similarly, the consistency of the gender variable in the GUAS case, though not significant, might result from an omission of key control variables like the semester the exam is taken. Since, in both situations, Model 3 reports almost the same coefficients for the gender variable as long as the full data sets are considered. One possible reason could be that in the GUAS case the coefficient reflects on the actual effect of gender from the outset, while in the GU case controls for existing differences in the exams are required to reveal the true impact of gender.

Adding to these first insights in a second step, the two data sets are merged. While this eliminated the chance to work with any controls, it provided the chance to considers the effect of gender within a private-public or rather a university vs. university of applied sciences dichotomy. To study in more detail how these two aspects interact, a two-factor variance analysis has been conducted. To assure comparability only those students are considered that passed the exam.

Table 3 reveals that the direct effect of the type of university as well as the interaction term - men at a private university - report significant effects. However, the effect of gender is insignificant. This results from a disordinal effect of gender.

Table 3 Variance Analysis - Combined Approach
Source: Own presentation

Variables	Coefficient
Gender	0.420
Type of University	61.302***
Interaction	36.131***
Constant	198,026.735***
R^2	0.002
Overall Model	92.830***

Looking at the effect of the type of university and the interaction effect in more detail, it shows that private universities of applied science are approximately 0.16 marks or 0.8 points worse than public universities. The interaction effect illustrates, that it is men at private universities of applied sciences that report even worse than the average, i.e. 0.2 grades or 1 point worse. These differences, even though they are significant, are of such a small size that the real difference in performance can almost be disregarded. Considering that at this point no controls are implemented, these results complement those for Model 1 from Table 1 and Table 2.

This final result additionally indicates that in a comparison of the two types of universities the preconception that good grades at universities of applied sciences and in particular private ones are worth less since it is perceived easier to get them does not necessary seem to hold – admitting to a potential bias potential bias due to preselection by the students in selecting the type of university they select based on their skill levels, which however cannot be analyzed herein. The results for the interaction effect, in particular, illustrate that women, even if only slightly, seem to do better in an environment with more personal interactions and stronger student supervision which is usually the case in private universities of any kind.

Summarizing, it can be seen that as soon as additional outside effects are controlled for which could also be the type of university any effect of gender vanishes, leading us to the conclusion that in the last decades in Germany the field of economics experienced gender equality in terms of exam results and neither women nor men report on average better or worse. In both approaches the third model including additional controls reports an insignificant effect of the gender that independent of the type of university levels off at roughly 0.12. However, this result only holds if the full data sets are considered, which would mean comparing only passing grades in the GUAS case with all possible outcomes in the GU case. If both models are estimated comparably it can be seen that the effect of gender in the GU case is even less pronounced than in the GUAS case. The reason for this difference is suspected in the missing semester dummy variables in the GUAS case.

As this study combined the insights from a public university and a private university of applied sciences, it can also be assumed that it captures a significant part of the German sector of tertiary education and allows for the results to representative for a significant share of the German academic sphere.

6   Conclusions

6.1   General Insights

The decades long discussion whether significant differences exist between the two genders in regard to their achievements in tests focusing on basic economics has been revisited in this paper. In contrast to but a few of the existing publications, real exam results from a German public university's macroeconomics classes and from a German private university of applied science's introductory economics classes - both for the most part first semester courses have been implemented to study the question. Therefore, the present study offers results based on data that did not result from artificial tests but from real exams. Additionally, it is the first study where the effect of gender is analyzed for German participants. The distinction between public and private, as well as universities and universities of applied science offers furthermore insights into the German tertiary education landscape.

Only in the GU case, the baseline model hints at a slightly superior performance by men. As soon as external factors are controlled for, any relevance of gender as an impact factor vanishes. Additionally, the effects of both universities level off at the same

Perret, Jens K.:
On the Gender Performance Gap in Economics Education -
A Comparison of German Public and Private Universities

marginal level (model 3) hinting at a marginal effect of gender in German tertiary education independent of the type of university considered.

6.2   Policy Recommendation

Considering that almost a decade of student data has been evaluated, it can be assumed that the equality of men and women with regard to their economics education already is deeply entrenched in the German tertiary education system. While the results of this study do not imply that the situation of men and women in economics education is the same, it shows on the one hand that regarding outcomes differences can no longer be detected.

On the other hand, the robustness check using indicators of the students' cultural background indicated that a significant difference between different backgrounds might exists. In the implemented data sets it has been in particular students with a migratory background that reported slightly worse results in their exams then 'German' students; for students with Turkish or Middle Eastern backgrounds the difference has even been significant.

Summarizing the last two paragraphs from an educational policy point of view, a focus on a stronger integration and support of students with migratory backgrounds should be at the forefront of education policy.

6.3   Limitations and Outlook

While the study offers new and interesting insights for German public universities and private universities of applied sciences the question whether the results in the third main form of German tertiary education, i.e. public universities of applied sciences report comparable results. A fourth option as in private universities might complement the picture, but due to their small relevance for the German tertiary education system are not of foremost relevance.

Additionally, the biggest advantage of this study also is the source of it most pronounced limitations. Since real exam data is considered from two different institutions with differing testing environments and regulations it has not been possible to source a large number of comparable characteristics of the students. This holds to a slightly lower degree for each institution on its own. The results of the analyses show in particular that a significant number of relevant characteristics are still missing from the analysis.

Additional insights could result from using the same methodology on students' exam results from other countries; aside from the European abroad and the US; it might be of particular interest to consider countries where women's situations at universities and in society in general are not as established as in the Western world. This type of comparative analysis also would not only provide valuable insights but as well an empirical basis for policies addressing gender equality in tertiary education. It would also expand upon the role of the cultural background of the students only touched upon in this study.

While this article motivates that no significant differences exist between the gender when considering economics as a general basics lecture which is part of many a study program, it does not say anything about their performance in more sophisticated lectures and different fields of study. Additionally, in this article it has been argued that differences across study programs especially in the GUAS case can be disregarded due to the university structure. This assumption could be studied in more detail by focusing on other courses and study performance in general.

In a similar direction the question would go whether the teaching style of the lecturer does impact the student's performance and in far do gender differences result from different teaching styles.

Since the study is based on data from before the COVID 19 pandemic and the related lockdowns, which for most German universities resulted in cancellation of lectures or teaching at a distance, a very important questions would be in how far the results of this study hold for the years of the pandemic and the time afterwards when universities started to open again.

Finally, since the results do not indicate significant gender differences in German the outcomes of German economics exams, studies with a focus on economics education per se are required to be mirrored with a German focus to see what makes German students, independent of their gender, achieve better academic results in the field of economics instead of focusing on the gender issue alone.

Acknowledgements

The author would like to thank Sonja Beer for the impetus to this article and the anonymous reviewer for the helpful comments.

Data Availability

The implemented data set is available upon reasonable request.

Perret, Jens K.:
On the Gender Performance Gap in Economics Education -
A Comparison of German Public and Private Universities

References

Antecol, H.; Eren, O.; Ozbeklik, S. (2015): The Effect of Teacher Gender on Student Achievement in Primary School. In: Journal of Labor Economics, 33. (2015), No. 1, pp. 63–89.

Arnold, I.; Wietske, R. (2014): First-year study success in economics and econometrics: The role of gender, motivation, and math skills. In: The Journal of Economic Education, 45. (2014), No. 1, pp. 25–35.

Attiyeh, R.; Lumsden, K. (1971): University students' initial understanding of economics: The contribution of the A level economics course and of other factors. In: Economica, 38. (1971), No. 149, pp. 81–97.

Bach, G.; Saunders, P. (1965): Economic education: Aspirations and achievements. In: The American Economic Review, 55. (1965), No. 3, pp. 329–356.

Bach, G.; Saunders, P. (1966): Lasting effects of economics courses at different types of institutions. In: The American Economic Review, 56. (1966), No. 3, pp. 505–511.

Ballard, C.; Johnson, M. (2005): Gender, expectations, and grades in introductory microeconomics at a US university. In: Feminist Economics, 11. (2005), No. 1, pp. 95–122.

Becker, W.; Watts, M. (2001): Teaching economics at the start of the 21st century: Still chalk-and-talk. In: American Economic Review, 91. (2001), No. 2, pp. 446–451.

Buckles, S.; Freeman, V. (1983): Male-female differences in the stock and flow of economic knowledge. In: Review of Economics and Statistics, 65. (1983), No. 2, pp. 355–358.

Burns, J.; Halliday, S.; Keswell, M. (2012): Gender and risk taking in the classroom (Saldru Working Paper, vol. 87).

Chan, N.; Kennedy, P. (2002): Are multiple-choice exams easier for economics students? A comparison of multiple-choice and "equivalent" constructed-response exam questions. In: Southern Economic Journal, 68. (2002), No. 4, pp. 957–971.

Chudgar, A.; Sankar, V. (2008): The Relationship between Teacher Gender and Student Achievement: Evidence from five Indian States. In: Compare, 38. (2008), No. 5, pp. 627–642.

Ferber, M.; Birnbaum, B.; Green, C. (1983): Gender differences in economic knowledge: A reevaluation of the evidence. In: The Journal of Economic Education, 14. (1983), No. 2, pp. 24–37.

Gohmann, S.; Spector, L. (1989): Test scrambling and student performance. In: Journal of Economic Performance, 20. (1989), No. 3, pp. 235–238.

Heath, J. (1989): An econometric model of the role of gender in economic education. In: The American Economic Review, 79. (1989), No. 2, pp. 226–230.

Hedges, L.; Nowell, A. (1995): Sex differences in mental test scores, variability, and numbers of high-scoring individuals. In: Science, 269. (1995), No. 5220, pp. 41–45.

Hirschfeld, M.; Moore, R.; Brown, E. (1995): Exploring the gender gap on the GRE subject test in economics. In: The Journal of Economic Education, 26. (1995), No. 1, pp. 3–15.

Johnson, M.; Robson, D.; Taengnoi, S. (2014): A meta-analysis of the gender gap in performance in collegiate economics courses. In: Review of Social Economy, 72. (2014), No. 4, pp. 436–459.

Kaiser, T. (2020): Measuring economic competence of secondary school students in Germany. In: The Journal of Economic Education, 51. (2020), No. 3-4, pp. 227–242.

Kelley, A. (1975): The student as a utility maximizer. In: Journal of Economic Education, 6. (1975), No. 2, pp. 82–92.

Lumsden, K.; Scott, A. (1987): The economics student reexamined: Male-female differences in comprehension. In: The Journal of Economic Education, 18. (1987), No. 4, pp. 365–375.

MacDowell, M.; Senn, P.; Soper, J. (1977): Does sex really matter? In: The Journal of Economic Education, 9. (1977), No. 1, pp. 28–33.

Makridou-Bossiou, D. (2006): Gender differences in economic knowledge in Greece. In: International Business & Economics Research Journal, 5. (2006), No. 11, pp. 35–41.

Marin, C.; Rosa-Garcia, A. (2011): Gender bias in risk aversion: Evidence from multiple choice exams (MPRA Paper).

Perret, Jens K.:
On the Gender Performance Gap in Economics Education -
A Comparison of German Public and Private Universities

Mondak, J. J.; Anderson, M. R. (2004): The Knowledge Gap: A Reexamination of Gender-Based Differences in Political Knowledge. In: The Journal of Policy, 66. (2004), No. 2.

Myers, J. K.; Franklin, M. A.; Lepak, G. M.; Graham, J. F. (2018): The impact of gender and cognitive information processing models on CPA exam pass rates: A call for research. In: Journal of Business and Educational Leadership, 7. (2018), No. 1, pp. 59–71.

Oberrauch, L.; Kaiser, T. (2020): Economic competence in early secondary school: Evidence from a large-scale assessment in Germany. In: International Review of Economics Education, 35. (2020).

Rhine, S. (1989): The effect of state mandates on student performance. In: American Economic Review, 79. (1989), No. 2, pp. 231–235.

Roach, T. (2014): Student perceptions toward flipped learning: New methods to increase interaction and active learning in economics. In: International Review of Economics Education, 17. (2014), pp. 74–84.

Siegfried, J. (1979): Male-female differences in economic education: A survey. In: Journal of Economic Education, 10. (1979), No. 2, pp. 1–11.

Soper, J.; Walstad, W. (1988): What is high school economics? Posttest knowledge, attitudes, and course content. In: Journal of Economic Education, 19. (1988), No. 1, pp. 37–51.

Thompson, A. (2012): Do men and women perform differently on different types of test questions? (Conference Paper: Southern Agricultural Economics Association Annual Meeting).

Tonin, M.; Wahba, J. (2015): The Sources of the Gender Gap in Economics Enrolment. In: CESifo Economic Studies, 61. (2015), No. 1, pp. 72–94.

UniRank (2022): 2022 German University Ranking (https://www.4icu.org/de/). Accessed on 29.09.2022.

Walstad, W.; Soper, J. (1989): What is high school economics? Factors contributing to student achievement and attitudes. In: Journal of Economic Education, 20. (1989), No. 1, pp. 39–57.

Watts, M. (1987): Student gender and school district differences affecting the stock and flow of economic knowledge. In: Review of Economics and Statistics, 69. (1987), No. 3, pp. 561–566.

Watts, M.; Lynch, G. (1989): The principles courses revisited. In: The American Economic Review, 79. (1989), No. 2, pp. 236–241.

Wuthisatian, R. (2020): Student exam performance in different proctored environments: Evidence from an online economics course. In: International Review of Economics Education, 35. (2020).

Perret, Jens K.:
On the Gender Performance Gap in Economics Education -
A Comparison of German Public and Private Universities

Appendix

Variable	Description
Gender	0 - male
	1 - female
Type of University	0 - Private University of Applied Sciences
	1 - Public University
Semester of Student	Semester of Exam – Starting Semester of Student
2. Try	0 - No
	1 - Yes
3. Try	0 - No
	1 - Yes
Begin in Summer	0 - No
	1 - Yes
English Trail	0 - No
	1 - Yes
Dummies Program	Business Administration (Base)
	Social Sciencies
	Mathematics, Physics
	Engineering
Dummies Semester	Summer Semester 2007 – Winter Semester 2015/2016
	Winter Semester 2007 (Base)
Dummies Location	Dortmund (Base)
	Munich
	Hamburg
	Frankfurt
	Cologne
	Stuttgart
Dummies Year	2007-2017
	2007 (Base)

About the Author

Prof. Dr. Jens K. Perret studied business mathematics and eco-nomics at the University of Wuppertal. He received his PhD in economics on the knowledge society in Russia from the University of Wuppertal. Between 2004 and 2016, Mr. Perret worked at the European Institute for International Economic Relations, first as a student assistant and later as a research assistant. From 2007 to 2016, Mr. Perret was a research assis-  tant at the Chair of Macroeconomic Theory and Policy. From 2012 to 2014, he held teaching positions at the Kaliningrad University of Technology, among others. Since September 2016, he has been Professor of Economics and Statistics at the International School of Management in Cologne.

Perret, Jens K.:
On the Gender Performance Gap in Economics Education -
A Comparison of German Public and Private Universities

International School of Management

Die International School of Management (ISM) – eine staatlich anerkannte, private Hochschule – bildet seit 1990 in Dortmund, Frankfurt/Main, München, Hamburg, Köln, Stuttgart und Berlin Nachwuchsführungskräfte für die internationale Wirtschaft aus. Das Studienprogramm umfasst Vollzeit-Bachelor- und -Master-Studiengänge, duale, berufsbegleitende, MBA- und Fernstudiengänge sieben Vollzeit-Bachelor-Studiengänge, neun Vollzeit-Master-Studiengänge, einen fachfremden Master-Studiengang, einen vorbereitenden Pre-Master sowie drei duale Studiengänge und drei berufsbegleitende Programme (B.A. Business Administration, M.A. Management, MBA General Management). Alle Studiengänge der ISM zeichnen sich durch ihre Internationalität und Praxisorientierung aus. Diese Erfolgsfaktoren garantiert die ISM durch enge Kooperationen mit Unternehmen, Projekte in Kleingruppen sowie integrierte Auslandssemester und -module an weltweit ca. 190 Partnerhochschulen. Die Qualität der Ausbildung bestätigen Studierende und Ehemalige ebenso wie Personaler in zahlreichen Hochschulrankings. Die ISM belegt dort seit Jahren konstant vorderste Plätze.

Mit dem ISM Working Paper werden Ergebnisse von Arbeiten präsentiert, wie z. B. Thesen, Ergebnisse aus Workshops oder aus eigenen Forschungsarbeiten. Ähnlich wie beim ISM Research Journal, das ebenfalls zu den neuen ISM Publikationsreihen gehört, werden die Beiträge im ISM Working Paper einem fachlichen Bewertungsverfahren (Peer Review) unterzogen.

In der Reihe „Working Paper" bisher erschienen:

No. 1   Brock, Stephan; Antretter, Torben: Kapitalkostenermittlung als Grauzone wertorientierter Unternehmensführung, 2014

No. 2   Ohlwein, Martin: Die Prüfung der globalen Güte eines Kausalmodells auf Stabilität mit Hilfe eines nichtparametrischen Bootstrap-Algorithmus, 2015

No. 3   Lütke Entrup, Matthias; Simmert, Diethard; Tegethoff, Carolin: Die Entwicklung des Working Capital in Private Equity Portfolio-unternehmen, 2017

No. 4   Hampe, Lena; Rommel, Kai: Einflüsse von kognitiven Verzerrungen auf das Anlageverhalten deutscher Privataktionäre, 2017

No. 5   Lütke Entrup, Matthias; Simmert, Diethard; Caspari, Lisa: Die Performance von deutschen Portfoliounternehmen nach Private Equity Buyouts, 2017

No. 6   Brickau, R. A.; Cornelsen, J.: The impact of visual subliminal triggers at the point of sale on the consumers' willingness to purchase – A critical investigation into gender differences, 2017

No. 7   Hampe, L.; Rommel, K.: Einflüsse von kognitiven Verzerrungen auf das Anlageverhalten deutscher Privataktionäre, 2017

No. 8   Brickau, R. A.; Röhricht, J.: Archaische Gesten im POS-Marketing – Die Nutzung archaischer Gesten in der Display- und Plakatwerbung, 2017

No. 9   Fontanari, M.; Kredinger, D.: Risiko- und Resilienzbewusstsein. Empirische Analysen und erste konzeptionelle Ansätze zur Steigerung der Resilienzfähigkeit von Regionen, 2017

No. 10   Schröder, C.; Weber, U.: Integration von Flüchtlingen in den Arbeitsmarkt als Chance für Diversity Management: Einführung und ausgewählte Beispiele im Kreis Steinfurt, 2017

No. 11   Zimmermann, N. A.; Gericke, J.: Supply Chain Risiko-management – Analyse des Status Quo und neuer Entwicklungstendenzen, 2018

No. 12   Haberstock, P.; Weber, G.; Jägering, C.: Process of Digital Transformation in Medium-Sized Enterprises - an Applied Re-search Study, 2018

Perret, Jens K.:
On the Gender Performance Gap in Economics Education -
A Comparison of German Public and Private Universities

No. 13	Potaszkin, I.; Weber, U.; Groffmann, N.: „Die süße Alternative" Smart Health: Akzeptanz der Telemedizin bei Diabetikern, 2018
No. 14	Holthaus, L.; Horn, C.; Perret, J. K.: E-Commerce im Luxusmarken-segment – Die Sicht deutscher Kundinnen am Beispiel Chanel, 2020
No. 15	Bingemer, S.; Ohlwein, M.: Mit Customer Experience Management die Digitalisierung meistern – Die Rolle von Unternehmens-kultur und -organisation, 2020
No. 16	Gildemeister, C. C.; Mehn, A.; Perret, J. K.: Factory-Outlet-Center: Discount oder Disney?, 2021
No. 17	Böge, C.; Perret, J. K.; Netzel, J.: Die Effekte der Zielorientierung auf den Berufserfolg – Erste empirische Befunde, 2021
No. 18	Stotz, S.; Brickau, R. A.; Moss, C., Meierhof, D.: Measuring and Restoring customer trust - an explorative research based on the VW Diesel gate scandal, 2021
No. 19	Perret, J. K.: On the Gender Performance Gap in Economics Education - A Comparison of German Public and Private Universities, 2022